Sex Tells

By Darick "DDS" Spears

Sex Tells

Rated: 5 minute Orgasm

Written and "UN-Edited" by

Darick "DDS" Spears

Sex Tells

Copyright © 2015 by Darick Spears

ISBN 9780692547106

Printed in USA by DDS MediaWorks LLC./21st Century Shakespears Publishing

Sex Entries

The Disclaimer

This book contains graphic sexual content and is based on a true story. It is made to open up the world of sex, and the negativity it can have if used wrong. If you are ready to proceed then enter into the mind of Darick Spears and his new entry Sex Tells.

More books available by Darick Spears on Amazon:

#1 Bestseller
The Diary of a Stay-at-home Dad: My Journal Behind Bars

Dedication

This book is dedicated to all of those who struggle in their relationships, their daily spiritual walks, and much more!

Sex makes people so uncomfortable, but in many ways we need it to survive. We just have to learn to use it the way God intended it to be used for.

If you have further questions, contact DDS MediaWorks/21st Century Shakespears Publishing. Our regular business hours are Mon-Thurs. 8:30 am – 8 pm EST, and Friday 8:30 am – 5 pm. During these hours, you can reach us by phone, email or on-line chat. Outside of these hours, either call and leave a message or email us.

Phone: 414-628-0798
Email: darick@ddsmediaworks.com
Website: www.darickspears.com

Author Biography

Darick "DDS" Spears, is an artist, producer, business owner, certified audio engineer with experience in video/film production, and an author. He graduated from Marquette University Milwaukee, WI with a Bachelors in Communications and Minor in Intermediary Business 2000-2005. He got his Masters Degree in Music Business at Columbia College Chicago, IL 2006-2008.

He also received his Associate Degree in Recording & Video Technology from Madison Media Institute 2010-2012.

Darick is a Business owner. DDS MediaWorks LLC, Milwaukee, WI: is a tri-media company that deals with music production, video production, and book writing/publishing.

Under the DDS Mediaworks umbrella, is a music label called Elevator Muzik Group. This music label was founded and is ran by Darick Spears. Log on to www.darickspears.com to check out new music.

Finally, he has began a new book department called the 21st Century Shakespears Publishing Company. Known for the #1 Besteller book entitled : **The Diary of a stay-at-home Dad: My Journal Behind Bars**, *by Darick Spears. With the second installment entitled "***Sex Tells***," this company is on it's way to creating more books that deal with romance, poetry, business, spirituality, and much more.*

Prelude

Sex Tells takes its readers into a journey about sex and what it can do to a person's life. Sex is often looked at as a bad thing in society, but Darick looks at both sides of the issue and reveals real life situations and how they can either make or break someone.

This book is very sexual and descriptive, in "Darick Spears fashion." Thank you for supporting Darick, and please feel free to support his music, films, and other projects by visiting www.darickspears.com

"Everyone says that sex kills, but I believe it tells

a story like the one I am about to unfold." _DDS

CHAPTER ONE

THE ADVENT

THE ADVENT

It was a Wednesday night in July, and the weather equated to a room full of body oils and lit candles. The breeze smelled like a woman's fresh cleavage sprinkled with some Bath and Body Works body spray. Ice, who was an out of towner was visiting the city of Milwaukee on business.

He had just stepped off the Megabus and waltzed up the street to the Hilton located on 4t^h and Wisconsin. As he neared the check-in desk, he reached in his camouflage Ed Hardy shorts to find his wallet. Finally, finding it's locality he took out his ID

and credit card, and spoke,

" Hi, I reserved a room on hotwire and I need to

check- in."

Ice immediately took note of the hotel clerk who

was dark chocolate with the first three buttons of her

shirt open, displaying her beautiful cleavage.

"Tracy," the girl said abruptly, "that's my name if

you were wondering, and my bra size is 38 DD."

Ice could hardly get the words out as his dick

began to grow to a stiff point.

"Oh, thanks Tracy. Sorry I was looking at your

tits but they were just so intriguing at the moment."

Tracy and Ice exchanged looks then he received

his keys proceeding to the $4t^h$ floor to find room 415.

Tired and aroused at the same time from his encounter

at the front desk, Ice decided to take a 15 minute hot

shower, and then relax.

As Ice rested on the well-polished bed in his Hilton room, he heard the door open. Believing that it was all part of his imagination, he didn't respond and laid his head back onto his pillow. Restless, Ice heard another noise that caught his attention immediately. It was Tracy standing in front of him with her shirt open.

Her breasts were covered in baby oil, her nipples were hard, and she began to pull off his towel and caress his hard dick. Tracy took her tits and smothered Ice's penis in between them, stroking up and down.

As he moaned she took her tongue and licked around the head of his dick and she began to suck it while massaging his nuts. Ice was entering into a climax when he screamed, "I'm cumming, I'm cumming." Tracy took every bit of fluid that came out of his pipe, and then advanced to the door.

But before leaving she turned around and said, "Welcome to the Mil. Next time you'll get to see how my booty bounces from the back."

Astonished, he picked up his phone and called one his best friends from Milwaukee,

"Man, you would not believe what just happened. Come and get me, I'm at the Hilton you gotta show me some more of your city."

In a phase of contentment, Ice didn't even washed his dick that was just deep throated. Instead he put on some clothes, some cologne, and headed downstairs to meet up with his best friend Darnel.

Now, Darnel was a lady's man and he was born and raised in Milwaukee, so he knew the ends and outs. Ice was from Houston, and down south they did things a little different, but he was happy to be in Milwaukee.

He and Darnel had met through the music industry and Ice was in town to collaborate on a new track for Darnel's album. Darnel had a reputation as a well-known producer/rapper.

He was also working on a new movie and a book, so he had a lot of things on his plate and Ice could help him calm his mind. Finally, arriving to pick up his friend, Ice and Darnel went to Major Goolsbys to get some lunch.

"What's the deal my nigga? I see you already getting ya dick sucked. You in the Mil kid! It's official," Darnel screamed.

They both caught up and then proceeded to his crib to listen to some hot tracks for his album. As they finished recording their hot new single, Darnel warned Ice about the woes of the game, and that sex tells.

He was confused by what Darnel had said, because no one had ever conveyed that statement to Ice like that. As they headed back to his hotel, Ice took his friends warning as food for thought and when he got back to his room he fell asleep almost instantly.

"Sex tells," just kept repeating in his head and it would be a while before he could understand the phrase. It was about two knocks on his door, when Ice woke up and noticed that the morning sun was out.

He made his way to the door and as he opened it, standing in his boxers, to his surprise there was no one there. He then leaned his head out the door to see that it was just a couple of maids seeing if the room needed cleaning.

" Oh wow, what a first 24 hours in the Mil."

CHAPTER TWO

ROOM SERVICE

ROOM SERVICE

Last night Darnel had drove home reminiscent of the many years he had spent out on the streets messing with various "bout its." These were women who were down to do anything sexual, monetarily, and even violent at any moment when told to by Darnel. His dick got hard many times as he replayed scenes in a lustful manner.

Big booty girls walking around in thongs fixing the bed up ready to get tore down is all that he could imagine as his hormones rose. It got so bad that he pulled his car to the side of the road, reached in his glove compartment where he kept some lotion and began to stroke his penis to the rhythm of his imagination.

Finally, after cumin all over the steering wheel, he drove home to his family and went to bed.

He had been in a relationship with his baby mother for about four years and they had a beautiful son who was a mirror of his mother more than his father. Many times Darnel wondered what had happened to his relationship that made him so lustful of other women.

In fact, he even smiled at the fact that he had planted the lady at the hotel register to show his friend a good time. He was a mysterious man who feared God but constantly fought with his own sexual desires.

That night, as he laid in the bed next to his tired baby mama, Darnel thought about the many stories his sex would tell. Most women could tell what he was going though just by the way he hit it from the back, or the way his tongue would spin around her clitoris causing her to climax. He was an artistic man with Godly-fear and wisdom, but often felt trapped in a world of expectations.

People wanted so much from him as a person, and this caused him great hurt. But his mind was his only freedom. Darnel worked like a maniac, throwing his creativity into producing and recording albums, writing novels, poetry, and even directing and producing films.

His drive was given to him from God, as well as his talents, but this also called much backlash from his peers.

He was going through a point in his life that would someday be the turning point where the dark would turn into light.

CHAPTER THREE

TEACH YOU A LESSON

Teach You a Lesson

Ice woke up feeling quite relieved from his first day in the Mil which was full of exciting things. He was checked into a hotel and received great service from the sexy clerk.

Equally important, he met up with his best friend and got to make some classic music. Today could only be a guessing game for Ice, because he didn't' have a clue of what would be in store for him.

As he waltzed around his room in the nude, the sun radiated through the blinds and reflected off of his muscular physique. Music played from his computer, and out of the small speakers was Darnel's new mix tape playing.

As Ice played number 4 entitled "Pussy Patty." He listened to the lyrics of his best friend, who told a story about how pussy almost got him killed. Ice paused for a second to think about what he was listening to, and he soon realized that his friend was a man of wisdom.

"That nigga gone blow up one day watch," Ice repeated to himself as the music kept playing.

Within ten minutes he heard his phone ring and it was Darnel.

"Yo my nigga, I'm downstairs let's roll out."

He slipped on his outfit and headed down the stairs. As he hit the door exit he ran into a Puerto Rican petite girl with a fatty. Now a fatty is a big juicy butt, and Ice was taken aback by her presence to the point where he turned around twice, and noticed she had done the same.

"Only one life to live, " he said to himself as he turned around and she said,

"Tanya.That's my name and later on tonight my ass is all yours."

Ice yelled out his room number as he laughed hysterically, wondering how every beautiful girl in this hotel could be so friendly. As he hopped into Darnel's new Black Range Rover laced with 30 inch rims, he looked astonished.

"Dang nigga, why look so funny in the face?" Darnel said.

Ice went on to tell him about how pleased he was with the service that he had been getting from the ladies in Milwaukee. They both chatted about what the day would present and it would totally consist of helping sell dinners at Darnel's church.

He had been made a deacon at his church recently, and was on a path of cleaning up his life.

But one thing he learned quickly was that even in the church there were hoes, and his situations would lead him down the wrong path many times.

Last night on his way home he received a call from one of the missionary's at church, Shawna, who needed to be let into the church. Darnel, being a good deacon came and opened the door for her.

Also, as a good gentlemen he waited for her in the lobby while she went downstairs to count the offering from bible class. She called him in the basement to ask him a few questions about how things had been going with his family.

He noticed that her shirt was unbuttoned a little bit, but it was hot so he thought nothing of it. As they talked more and more he could not help but to look down her shirt viewing her large caramel breast glisten from sweating a little bit.

She had long black hair and an innocent face. She was also married with a husband who did not appreciate her, and his constant cheating did not sit well with her.

Darnel's hormones were rising as the conversation picked up, to the point that he had to get up and walk to the bathroom.

As he stood up his large dick was budging out of his pants and Shawna had noticed. Immediately, her pussy got so wet that she had to go to the bathroom herself to take off her underwear.

Her nipples were so hard she had to stand for a minute, and even contemplated putting tissue inside her bra to keep them sustained. But she disregarded.

He finally got his dick to go down by pouring a little cold water down his pants. He knew that he was wrong to be lusting for a married woman, for it was against the bible, but this temptation was strong.

As he walked back to the office where they were having their conversation, he was aroused by her scent and turned around to find her coming out of the bathroom at the same moment.

Shawna had a look in her eyes that told a story. She wanted Darnel so bad to just kiss her soft lips and caress her butt, while taking his tongue and circling around her nipples. On the other hand, he wanted Shawna to massage his dick while licking his neck and ears.

At that instant, they were both considered sinners because in their minds the iniquity had been committed. The outcome was that of a church hoe story.

Darnel unbuttoned Shawna's shirt with his teeth, after gently biting her neck and massaging her cleavage with his tongue. Shawna had an orgasm just standing up and as her breast were getting soaked in his sweet tongues saliva, she slide her hands down his pants caressing his anaconda.

They were both like two wild animals as he bent Shawna over the church counter in the basement and hit her from the back. She retaliated by throwing him on a chair and riding him until he whispered her name in her ear.

Then he stood up and she fell to her knees in prayer position, and sucked his children out of his dick. Immediately after this episode the guilt was there, but also there was a smile of contentment.

Both of them knew this fling could not last for long, because they were both married and both knew each other's spouse.

After Darnel told Ice this story, he was hard thinking about this woman he had never met. Ice realized that the game of temptation never stops, but he was proud of Darnel for walking the straight and narrow; even if he had slipped a few times.

All of these paths that lead down the road of life can be told all in one lesson of sex. Sex is one of the most powerful tools that can trigger man and woman's emotions positively, but it can also be used as a negative one.

"Have you ever heard of a sex slave?" he asked Ice.

He replied "No."

Darnel warned him not to ever become one.

CHAPTER FOUR

GRADE "A" PUSSY

GRADE "A" PUSSY

Ice and Darnel finished up their conversation and began to tone it down as they arrived at the church. This church was not that big from the outside, but upon entrance it was grand.

Darnel respected his elders so he took his Milwaukee Brewers baseball cap off, and his two sterling silver earrings out as well. Ice followed suit, and as he walked downstairs he noticed two things.

The male mind works odd when he notices two beautiful women, because they become sexual objects instantly; and in all cases it's not a bad thing. This is because women do it too.

As Ice entered the basement of the church, two girls Tanya and Cherry both took notice and were aroused, as his body in their minds, turned into a big dick.

They introduced themselves to him and from the intro Ice noticed that Tanya and Cherry were very friendly. He explained that he was visiting from out of town and was staying downtown in the Hilton.

The girls seemed so intrigued and told him they would love to come and visit, and also show him around town. They exchanged numbers and Ice was so excited about his two new gorgeous admirers.

As he headed out of the church, the name Tanya reminded him of the Puerto Rican girl who was at the hotel earlier, who had promised him a piece of ass. Ice felt like it was truly his lucky week and excitement danced within his body.

Darnel understood everything that was going on with his friend but he had problems of his own.

His mind kept tap dancing with thoughts of Shawna and the night before. What was the reason for this strange attraction and episode that newly surfaced? Darnel was finding out that it's harder to walk the straight and narrow then it is to walk the wide.

When an individual doesn't care about their soul it's easier to do whatever they want to do without guilt, but the second that person decides to do the right thing then it seems like every piece of temptation is thrown rapidly.

At this point, Ice could not understand this because he was walking the wide path, and tonight would be full of adventure.

CHAPTER FIVE

IF WALLS COULD

TALK

If Walls Could Talk

This night would hold surprises for both Darnel and Ice.

First off, on his way home, Darnel received a text message from Shawna, that asked him to stop by her house because she was desperately in need of help.

His stomach sank with nervousness and rose with excitement, because he was in deep hopes that she was alright, and at the same time happy to see her.

As he neared her home he noticed that there were no cars in front of the house, so he wondered was she at home yet? As he rang the door bell, he checked to make sure he was smelling fresh and looking good.

He had an all white t-shirt that fit his muscular physique, some Girbaud shorts and a pair of all white Dookies, which most people call Nike Air Force Ones.

As he turned to get ready to leave, the door opened and it was Shawna wearing a robe and looking beautiful as ever.

She seemed to be in a rush as she opened the door and gave him a quick welcome hug. Then she rushed into the only room in the house with a light on. His first thought was where were her husband and kids?

At the very same moment Shawna yelled, "Come in and make yourself at home. My hubby and kids are out of town visiting his mom." He instantly felt relieved but still curious of what this emergency was all about. His clothes still wreaked of Shawna's body spray and it was turning him on.

Darnel entered into her guest room where she was sitting on the bed watching TV. Shawna looked up at him and smiled as she lifted the remote to turn the TV off.

"I have to ask you a question, well more like a favor," she sighed.

"What is it?" Darnel said.

Shawna went on to tell Darnel about her aspirations of being a model and she wanted him to choose her poses and outfits. He agreed and was at ease because he thought the emergency was something much worst.

Shawna took off her black robe and she was laced with a black bra that was see through, and a black thong accompanied by a pair of black pumps. Her double d's were soaked in oil and her beautiful butt cheeks were also glistening and moved like a bowl of jelly.

Darnel almost lost his mind when Shawna laid across the floor and looked into his eyes while asking,

"How is this pose?"

His dick jumped up like a stressed person's blood pressure, and he said,

" I think you should do it like that but position your butt different, also maybe show some more cleavage."

Shawna got up, put one leg up on the bed and took off her bra.

"Is this better?" she asked.

Her tits sat perfectly against her thorax and Darnel lost it. He reached over and pulled Shawna's thong to the side, he began to lick her clit from the back. He then took his tongue and stroked it in and out of her pussy listening to her moan.

Shawna took her body and spun it around so that her face was in between his crotch. She unzipped his pants with her teeth, and out popped his 11 inch dick and she deep throat every inch of it. They were animals who were both deprived within their relationships. Their sins that night were felt to be justified by their situations.

Darnel was not happy with his unappreciative lady and Shawna was fed up with her cheating husband. Both were in the wrong but enjoying every second of it.

Shawna got on top on his pole and began to ride him as Darnel sucked her tits like a new born baby searching for milk. He then spread her legs from side to side as she rested on her stomach and worked her out from behind.

He began to spank her butt cheeks and as he got close to his climax she screamed,

"Im cumming."

Not being able to hold in his passion he replied,

" I'm cumming."

Shawna reached for his nuts and squeezed them making his nut squirt out even more. They both sang in unison and the session ended with a kiss, a hug, and an

"I will see you Sunday at church."

The sins of a trying deacon and missionary had reached a bad point. Darnel thought about how his road was getting harder but he vowed to not have sex with Shawna again.

Likewise, Shawna cried that night and asked God for strength and she vowed to stay away from Darnel as she walked on her straight and narrow.

Both of them went their ways knowing that they would eventually have to see each other at church, but while they were away their strength could be rejuvenated.

CHAPTER SIX

DOUBLE PARKED

Double Parked

Trying to escape the clutch of lust, love, or attraction, seems impossible. Darnel could not keep his mind off Shawna. Was it the curiosity of where this thing could go?

Could they both just continue fulfilling each others sexual passions, without leaving their families? All of these things ran through his mind, but guilt tap danced inside his stomach.

The pressures of living correct while denying himself of fleshly pleasures, were beginning to make him feel sick. His spouse did not provide him with the sufficient amount of sexual pleasures.

This made him often feel like he wasn't enough for her. This is because most women who are into their man, would want to do whatever to please him. As in his case, it wasn't evident. His wife many times ignored his desires and focused on her career.

Shawna was his sexual pleaser. She wanted Darnel in every way, and perhaps this is the reason he felt so confused. In the same way, he represented to Shawna what she was missing in her relationship.

She was often overlooked, not desired, not pleased, and her spouse showed her no respect. He wondered, are people sometimes forced to enter into situations of infidelity by their partners?

Before marriage we take vows, and after the fact, a lot of times the vows are not fulfilled. The main one people say is violated during divorce is cheating. But do we ever look at the other ones that are not kept? Like through sickness, the vow of honoring and respecting, just to name a few?

Completely confused he prayed for strength, because he could feel it in the air that there were more events to come.

Now, jealousy is something to try to avoid when one is having a side relationship. This could complicate the situation even worst, because it violates the initial agreement.

Shawna and Darnel never made a verbal agreement, that this was just a sex thing, but he felt it was a no brainer. They both were married, and it was no need to try to make this relationship anything beyond sex.

However, things began to change when a new woman arrived on the scene.

CHAPTER SEVEN

Planet of The Apes

Planet of the Apes

Ashley was a beautiful white woman with a gorgeous smile, sexy eyes, and a stunning figure. She was built like an amazon.

She had triple d's, an ass that was plump and damn there perfect; and the first time her and Darnel locked eyes, she knew something would happen between the two someday.

She was an up and coming actress who was very hungry for work. When Darnel put out a post on Craigslist, that he was in search for models/actresses for a new role in his independent film, she was the first to send a resume.

After receiving the email, Darnel contacted Ashley and they agreed to meet for lunch to discuss the film.

Upon arrival, he was in his usual businessmind. Focused on putting his best foot forward with this film, in order to get his name better out there as a director and producer.

But when his eyes locked on Ashley, all he felt was heat inside his body. She was like no other woman he had saw. He didn't know if he wanted to shake her hand or hug her? He didn't know if he wanted to smile or kiss her?

She wore some black leggings with a plain white t-shirt. Her hair was in a pony tail, and she smelled as fresh as baby lotion. Even in her dressed down attire, she was as hot as they come. Darnel, noticed her pretty green eyes staring deeply into his brown eyes. Ashley, could hardly speak herself, because she felt the same way.

Darnel had a presence about him when he entered a room. It's like he commanded attention. Perhaps it was because he actually didn't like much attention at all, that people took immediate notice of him.

Finally, he spoke, "Hi, Ashley. It's great to finally meet you!"

She replied, "Hi, Darnel. It's great to finally meet you as well!"

They both sat down and began to discuss each others ambitions and goals. Ashley was attracted to how passionate Darnel was about his plans for the future.

He explained to her his ideas for the film. She was very excited and at the same time calm.

Darnel was attracted to her spiritual vibe.

She was almost polar opposite of him, and that was becoming the magnetic field. Her thong was wet as she delve into deeper conversation with Darnel.

It got to the point that she had to cut the meeting short and wanted to meet at a different time.

Ashley was in a relationship that was just boring. She had a usual schedule and there was no excitement in her life. It seemed like everything was predictable.

Her boyfriend was always at work, and she pretty much was at home with her daughter all of the time. She was aware of Darnel being married, and she respected that.

In the same way, he knew of her situation and he was just trying to keep everything in decency. Darnel took his business very seriously, but he knew this could get very deep if lines were crossed between he and Ashley.

They had passion that could split a room in half. It would only be a matter of time before they had cross paths again. They planned to meet up the following week.

Chapter Eight

Knee Deep

Knee Deep

Ashley returned home that night with nothing on her mind but her encounter with Darnel. She thought it was love at first site, and this made her scared because she always wanted to be in control of all things.

She laid in her bed and rubbed on her soft breast and began to stick her finger in her pussy. She was so horny that she had an orgasm in less than 20 seconds.

She rolled over on her pillow and fell asleep to the thoughts of her mouth around Darnel's erect dick.

Meanwhile, he had many problems of his own to take care of. Shawna was on chill, but he did not know how long this would last.

He went home and made love to his wife, but only visiualizing Ashley being the recipient of this passionate session. He came so hard, and rolled over on his pillow with a strange feeling of the unknown about Ashley.

"Could I be in love with this woman?" He asked himself over and over in his confused mind.

The next morning Darnel was on his way to the studio to record some new songs when he got a text message from Ashley.

"Hi." she wrote.

"Hey.." he repliied.

They began to text each other back and forth all day long, with playful messages.

Ashley was typically a homebody who didn't have many friends. She preferred to remain low-key and out of trouble. So, when she was around the house, it was always great to have a conversation with someone.

Darnel filled this void, because Ashley's boyfriend was always working.

Darnel, being always on the move, was pretty much to himself as well. He loved to chat via text, glide, or any other social networks available.

He asked Ashley what she was wearing, and playfully she explained that she just had on a thong and bra.

The conversation ended with her sending him a picture that wasn't too explicit but she was in her bra smiling. He was so hard that he pulled out his dick in his private studio and stroked his sausage until he finished all over his phone.

Wiping it all off, he sent her a pic he took earlier before jagging off. It was an imprint of his dick in his boxers. She fingered herself until she squirted all over the phone.

She wiped it all, and fell asleep with nothing but Darnel on her mind.

Now, Darnel felt like he was happy to have met Ashley, but what was to come he did not know??

Chapter Nine

Buggin Out

Buggin Out

Darnel hated his life. He often felt unappreciated at home, and it seemed like everyone around him he was suspcious of their loyalty. You see, some people only come around when they feel like you are heading in the right direction.

They are like blood suckers, craving off the next man's energy. He often wondered who was sincere in his life? This made him a little paranoid. But he sought out Christ for an understanding and direction.

His spirituality was very important to him, and fighting the flesh was impossible to do alone.

He knew that he needed Christ for direction. So, he traveled to the church house that particular morning to get some prayer in at the alter.

He was at peace because he was by himself, and he could ask the Lord for forgiveness and restoration.

Dealing with women can be a difficult task. Many of them send out the completely wrong vibes to men, and as they wink their eyes, flash their cleavage, or shake their butts; a man can receive this as they are totally interested.

When in actuality this could mean nothing at all in their minds. So, Darnel wanted to avoid all women and just focus on his career and his path with Christ.

He needed strength because he knew that he would have to cross paths with women daily. But what he really wanted was just "focus."

As he lay on the alter, he heard the church door open. It was Shawna and two other young ladies from the church. They were there to rehearse for a singing engagment that they had in a few weeks.

Darnel was surprised and thrown out of his focus. He spoke to the ladies and began to assemble all of his belongings, when he felt a tap on his shoulder.

Shawna gave him a smile and a hug. As he tried to fight smelling her beautiful skin, he was immediately erect and imbalanced.

He had to hurry out of church, before he sacrificed her pussy on the alter.

She kissed his neck and whispered, "I miss you."

After this Darnel melted like a thin piece of ice in a tall glass of water.

Eye captivating eye, and body too close in proximity, they pulled their magnetic force apart and went their separate ways.

Darnel went to his car and immediately received a text message from Shawna. It was a smiley face attached with a picture of her cleavage. He was bugging out!

Chapter Ten

Paranoia

Paranoia

Not getting to release sexual tensions on a daily, can become very problematic. Shawna and Darnel both had spouses, but both were deprived of sex.

Their attraction to one another was very dangerous, and it's a good thing that Shawna was with two of her friends when she saw him.

Otherwise, the inevitable would have happened.

Today, he had a meeting with Ashley and wanted to leave yesterday's encounter with Shawna behind him. That would not be hard to do, because Ashley was a a breath of fresh air, Darnel couldn't help but to breathe in.

They met at his private condo where his studio and office was. She wore a beautiful sun dress with nothing but a bra and thong underneath.

The tension between the two was so thick. The more they spoke to each other, the more they lusted. Ashley smelled so good that Darnel wanted to lay her on the table, and lick every part of her body.

In the same manner, Ashley wanted to tie Darnel up to the studio console and ride him, suck him, until he squirted everywhere. The paranoia of ever getting too deep in love escaped both of their minds as their passions came to a collision.

It all started when Ashley dropped something on the floor and when she bent over to get it, all Darnel saw was ass and a red thong. He lost it.

He put his face in her ass and began to lick her pussy from behind. He juices dripped down his tongue and greased his face. She moaned and came within a minute.

Then, Ashley pulled out Darnel's cock and sucked it for 35 seconds and he exploded in her mouth. It was such a passion between the two that they didn't even care if they both came in less than a minute.

Each stared into the next one's eyes until they both fell asleep on the floor of the studio. An instrumental from Darnel's album just played on repeat for 3 hours.

As they both woke, realizing that getting home was important; they exchanged kisses, squeezes, and smiles, before leaving. Paranoia can creep up on you in the midst of uncertainty.

In this case, there was much fickleness in the air between Ashley and Darnel. All they both knew, was that they were falling for each other.

Chapter Eleven

Sexting

Sexting

Ashley returned home floating on cloud nine. She took a shower and put on a thong. She sprayed a rose scent body perfume on herself and began to apply lotion. In the middle of her after shower ritual, she reached for the phone and took a picture of her clitoris.

She sent the photo to Darnel and said she was waiting for him. Meanwhile, he was in the middle of a session, and once he saw the picture he had to to a 15-minute break.

Darnel went to the bathroom and his phone beeped again.

The message from Ashley said, "I want you to fuck me in my ass."

He instantly replied, "can I cum in you asshole?"

She sent a smiley face back and said, "How bout you cum in my ass and in my pussy."

The dark path had opened it's mouth for the both of them, and the straight and narrow was beginning to disappear.

This is what Darnel was trying to avoid, but one thing he could not stop was the fact that sin was everywhere. He had vowed to get out of the game, but something kept pulling him back in. It had to be the pussy.

Ashley was blinded from her own righteous path, because love and lust had devoured her heart. Now the two were in the midst of a modern day Babylon.

They planned to meet at a hotel later that night, and what happened was that of a baby making session.

She sucked Darnels dick, balls, while he licked her clit and ass. Then when the session was over he left her pussy full of cum, and they held each other with every minute being the most precious.

Chapter Twelve

The Encounter

The Encounter

As Darnel checked out of the hotel he floated to his car deep in love and lust. Shawna was far away from his mind, but she was even closer physically.

It just so happened that she was on her way to the same exact hotel to check in. She had a big fight with her husband and was in need of a break.

As Darnel opened his door to get into his car, he heard a voice say,

"Hey. What are you doing here?"

Immediately, his love high disappeared and he fumbled to find the right words but came up with

"Um, nothing. Had a conference in the hotel yesterday."

As they conversed back and forth, he failed to notice that Ashley was coming out of the hotel and she approached him saying,

"I'll talk to your later sweetie."

She kissed him on the cheek and his heart almost jumped out of his shirt.

"Goodbye Ashley, I will call you later."

There was no way that he could escape the confrontation he was about to have with Shawna. She looked so shocked and embarrased at the same time.

But she did something that was awkward. She just walked away without a fight, and said,

"Lord, I just don't have time for this shit today."

Ashley was in such a high herself off love that she didn't even notice Shawna, as she hopped in her car and pulled off.

Darnel waited for Ashley to pull off and followed after Shawna to make sure she was ok.

She said, "When were you going to tell me about that bitch?"

Her church oriented demeanor had left her at that moment of anger as Darnel asked if they could talk. He even paid for her room and they sat face to face disgusting issues that were going on between the both of them.

As she spoke he realized how much he missed her and how much he was still in love with her. Distance makes the heart grow fonder, and in this case Shawna also missed Darnel just as much.

She went into the bathroom and got a shower. As the water trickled down her curvy body, the tears intertwined with the shower water. Darnel couldn't hold in his own emotions, and walked into the bathroom to see if she was ok?

Shawna just cried and he couldn't do much but take his clothes off and get into the shower with an attempt to hold her. The passion was too thick and they made love from the shower to the bed room.

She kissed his neck, he kissed her forehead, her breast, and caressed her juicy ass. By the time they were down they woke up the next day. It was like paradise for both of them, and nothing in the world existed but the two of them.

Darnel was so caught up in his crazy world that he forgot to check on his friend Ice. Ice was enjoying himself as well. He was hanging with a few new girls that he met and this was not uncommon for the two to not speak for a week or so, especially when life got busy.

Ice had other business going on for himself in Milwaukee, so he wasn't mad when Darnel had to take care of his own matters. But things would change very soon for the two.

Chapter Thirteen

Pandora's Box

Pandora's Box

Now prior to Ice coming to Milwaukee, his life was dull and not full of sexual adventures. He felt like it was a lucky week for him, or maybe he didn't know that Darnel has set it up to be that way. You see, years ago, Darnel was visiting Ice in Texas and he did the ultimate "no, no."

This would consist of him sleeping with his Ice girlfriend while staying under his roof. Darnel felt very guilty so he secretly vowed to make it up to him, because if he ever found out their friendship would be over.

But one could wonder how Darnel got these women to do these things for him?

The answer lies in his sex. Many people become blind once they find the right partner that can play with their strings like a puppet. He had mastered the art of sex and with this power he could basically tell any woman he ever had relations with, to do him deeds.

In this, it would be to have sex with his best friend and treat him like he was the man.

Every minute and hour seemed to be going perfect that week, and even though Darnel was on a different path then that one he left in his past, Shawna and Ashley were bringing back his sex spirit seven times stronger.

That evening as he was driving alone he got an urge to call one of his old "bout its," and he fought the feeling as he drove home and went into his studio to produce his new album, "Rebel of tha Church." He vowed to tell the world the truth about the hard times of walking on the straight path, and why it was better than the wide ways.

But Ice on the other hand, was met at his hotel room door by the Puerto Rican girl named Tanya who had already been in his room waiting. As he attempted to open the door she quickly took the job of cracking it, and waltzing around the room with nothing but a pink thong which seemed to be non-existent within her fatty.

Her butt jiggled to the rhythm of his hormones and he noticed that the lights were dim and candles were lit. Ice was over the top with emotion and he came in his pants.

Tanya smiled because she knew that her ambiance caused this reaction, but she also knew her mouth could do wonders.

She pulled Ice to the bed and told him to hop in the shower for a couple minutes to clean up and get ready for her to suck his dick. As he walked toward the bathroom he noticed that it was one candle lit and water already running. He entered into a hot fog and took his clothes off.

As he entered the shower he thought that he heard more voices in the room so he put his ear to the door as he quietly closed it.

It was three voices in the room and one of them spoke,

" Let's just make this nigga cum and leave, so that daddy can be pleased with our work."

Ice thought to himself, "who is daddy?" Another voice said,

"Darnel is my baby and I would do anything for him, that's the only reason I'm sucking and fucking his friend."

Ice felt confusion and anger enter his body as he began to recollect about the whole week and why everything seemed so odd from the first day he got off the Mega Bus. He locked the bathroom door and just sat in the bath tub full of mixed emotions.

The shower water drizzled down his body but it could not wash away his confusion for the moment.

"Why would Darnel send all these women to do these things for me, and if he's a changed man how is still getting these favors done for free?"

The church hoes, the girl at the counter, the Puerto Rican girl, all just ran through his mind. Ice finally got up the nerves to turn the shower water off and tell Tanya that he's not feeling well and he won't be leaving the bathroom anytime soon.

She and the other two voices continued talking as they departed the room.

Ice took the first flight out that night without notifying Darnel, and he continued to evaluate his trip within his mind.

"Welcome to Pandora's box," is all that he could say to himself.

Chapter Fourteen

Point of No Return

Point of No Return

As Ice took an emergency flight back to Houston, instead of taking a few Mega buses, he had hopes to let the air clear before engaging in any conversations.

Meanwhile, Darnel went on avoiding Shawna, Ashley, and everything else that was negative in his path. He could not reach Ice and figured that he would call him sooner or later once he settled back down in Houston.

A few weeks passed by and Darnel felt pretty good about his life at that point. He felt like Ice enjoyed himself and he and Shawna would not be bumping heads anymore. Also, Ashley was supposedly on vacation with her boyfriend in Miami. He and his baby mother were doing very well, and even though they were married, he only referred to her as such.

This was because at the time their relationship wasn't going well, but now they were at good terms. It seemed as if nothing could go wrong as the months went by and Darnel was elevating his game in music, in his movie career, and even his writing as an author.

He still had not heard from Ice but he was used to this because they would talk every three months anyways.

Unfortunately, on this rainy Friday night in June this would all change. Darnel was driving home when he received a call from an unknown number, as he picked it up the phone he heard a voice crying.

"Hello. Hello," he said.

There was no response and just as he was getting ready to pull the phone from his ear he heard two words that would change his world forever, "I'm pregnant."

NOW AVAILABLE FROM
Darick DDS Spears !!!

Book (s)
Purchase Online (Amazon, Createspace, Kindle)

Personal Orders:
Email: darick@ddsmediaworks.com

The Diary of A Stay-at-home Dad: My Journal Behind Bars

Music (Albums)
Available: Itunes, Amazon, Cdbaby

The World is Yourz

The One Love Project

91

TO ORDER PRODUCT Send Email to
<u>darick@ddsmediaworks.com</u>

For the latest in creativity visit

www.darickspears.com